Find Your Future in Technology

Diane Lindsey Reeves

Created and produced by
Bright Futures Press, Cary, North Carolina
www.brightfuturespress.com

Published by
Cherry Lake Publishing, Ann Arbor, Michigan
www.cherrylakepublishing.com

Photo Credits: cover, Shutterstock/William Bradberry; cover, Shutterstock/Therrapol Pong Kangsananan; cover, Shutterstock/nicoelnino; cover, Shutterstock/imredesiuk; cover, Shutterstock/pogonici; page 4 (top), Shutterstock/Design Prax; page 4 (left), Shutterstock/johavel; page 6 (top), Shutterstock/William Bradberry; page 6 (left), Shutterstock/Porntep Naprasert; page 7, Shutterstock/lineartestpilot; page 8, Shutterstock/Maksin Dubinsky; page 9 (top), Shutterstock/pogonici; page 9 (left), Shutterstock/Zorandim; page 10, Shutterstock/Macrovector; page 11, Shutterstock/Stockimo; page 12 (top), Shutterstock/nicoelnino; page 12 (left), Shutterstock/Calavision; page 13, Shutterstock/Praneat; page 14, Shutterstock/Valeri Potapova; page 15 (top), Shutterstock/kentoh; page 15 (left), Shutterstock/andyOman; page 16, Shutterstock/moonkin; page 17, Shutterstock/bleakstar; page 18 (top), Shutterstock/studiovin; page 18 (left), Shutterstock/AG-PHOTOS; page 19, Shutterstock/vectomart; page 20, Shutterstock/Rawpixel.com; page 21 (top), Shutterstock/mangpor2004; page 21 (left), Shutterstock/Nata-Lia; page 22, Shutterstock/Aniwhite; page 23, Shutterstock/Monkey Business Images; page 24 (top), Shutterstock/ imredesiuk; page 24 (left), Shutterstock/Login; page 25, Shutterstock/VectorGoddess; page 25, Shutterstock/Tomacco; page 26, Shutterstock/ktsdesign; page 27 (top), Shutterstock/Therrapol Pong Kangsananan; page 27 (left), Shutterstock/Nikoloy Solidcreature; page 28, Shutterstock/JSlavy; page 29, pixabay.

Editorial Contributor: Kelly White

Library of Congress Cataloging-in-Publication Data

Names: Reeves, Diane Lindsey, 1959- author.
Title: Find your future in technology / by Diane Lindsey Reeves.
Description: Ann Arbor, Michigan : Cherry Lake Publishing, [2016] | Series:
  Find your future in STEAM | Audience: Grade 4 to 6. | Includes index.
Identifiers: LCCN 2016006587| ISBN 9781634718998 (hardcover) | ISBN
  9781634719452 (pbk.) | ISBN 9781634719223 (pdf) | ISBN 9781634719681
  (ebook)
Subjects: LCSH: Engineering--Vocational guidance--Juvenile literature.
Classification: LCC TA157 .R3853 2016 | DDC 602.3--dc23
LC record available at https://lccn.loc.gov/2016006587

Printed in the United States of America.

Table of Contents

Find Your Future in Technology

Find your future in technology

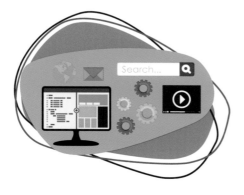

Hello, **digital native**! Yes, that means you, reader. Yours is the very first generation in history to be born into a high-tech world. You use technology to play video games, watch movies, and do homework.

You may not know it, but there is a world out there called "Information Technology," or IT for short (each letter pronounced "I–T"). Exciting opportunities exist for kids interested in computers and all kinds of technology! Soon there will be too many IT jobs and not enough IT workers!

Things like artificial intelligence, nanotechnology, and **robotics** bring game-changing discoveries. Expect big surprises ahead in everything from entertainment and business, to medicine and transportation.

This book—and the entire *Find Your Future* series—is for kids who like computers and digital gadgets and want to explore how people use IT at work. Some people even use technology to make the world a better place. Read on and imagine, if you can, the opportunities waiting for digital natives like you!

In each of the following chapters you will find three activities that you can do to dig deeper into the subject matter:

Surf the 'Net!

Type the words in **bold** into your favorite Internet search engine (like Google, Bing, or Yahoo) to find more information about the subject. Be sure to have permission and SUPERVISION from a trusted adult (like a teacher or parent) when using the Internet.

Explore Some More!

The Internet offers terrific resources to explore the world around you—in websites, in the news, and even in fun, online games. Here's your chance to goof around and learn some more!

Ask Big Questions!

Curiosity opens the door to learning (and fun!). Ponder the questions posed here. Each question comes with an activity idea so you can share your answers with others through posters, games, presentations, or even a good discussion where you consider both sides of an issue.

**Go online to download free activity sheets at
www.cherrylakepublishing.com/activities.**

Artificial Intelligence Scientist

Surf the 'Net!

Search for **IBM**, **Watson Jeopardy! videos**. Watch a smart computer taking on humans in a game of *Jeopardy!*

Artificial intelligence is everywhere you look. People use it in big and small ways every day. You use it when you get cash from a bank's ATM (automated teller machine). You use it when you watch computer-animated movies. You use it when you play video games, like Minecraft and SimCity.

Artificial intelligence, or AI, is asking **Siri** or **Cortana** for local movie times. AI is using **GPS** to find directions for a field trip. Facebook uses AI technology to analyze and describe photos, so a visually impaired person can "see." In a word, AI is awesome!

Even so, scientists are just starting to figure out all that artificial intelligence can do. It is one of the brave new frontiers of science, and the possibilities are very exciting!

Artificial intelligence scientists are very specialized technology engineers who teach computers to remember and mimic human-like behavior. Computers are not humans. They do not have emotions. They can't come up with new ideas or make decisions.

Computers have to be "programmed," to be told exactly what to do and how to do it. That's what artificial intelligence experts do.

To teach computers, scientists and technological engineers use "rules," like models, databases, and **algorithms** to tell computers how to act or respond with different commands. These rules teach things like computers, robots, and cell phones how to analyze responses and adapt, or "think," like a very smart person. As it turns out, computers can be very good students.

Ask Big Questions!

Can computers become smarter than humans? Some scientists worry it could happen someday. Others say "no way," because the human brain is far too complex to program into a machine. Answer the question by drawing a picture showing the world as either a better or a worse place thanks to robots.

Explore Some More!

Challenge your computer to a game of Rock-Paper-Scissors at **www.nytimes.com/interactive/science/rock-paper-scissors.html**.

It takes extremely smart people to teach computers to be smart. To make AI possible, artificial intelligence scientists must know a lot about math, science, and technology. They also have to understand how people think and how the human brain works.

No one knows for sure where AI will take us in the future, but experts have high hopes for good things to come. Using AI to control driverless cars is one idea where testing is already in high gear. Research shows that cars driven by AI instead of humans might drastically reduce, or even eliminate, traffic accidents.

Now that's smart science!

Artificial intelligence is used in manufacturing to make products more efficiently.

Biotechnology Engineer

Surf the 'Net!

Catch up with the latest innovations by searching for **biotechnology and you** or **biotechnology for kids**.

Biotechnology involves mixing technology with biology—the study of nature. Take, for example, those hooks-and-loop straps you use to fasten your shoes. You probably know them as Velcro™. Did you know Velcro™ was inspired by nature?

It's true! In the 1940s, a Swiss engineer named George de Mestral was walking with his dog in the woods when he noticed burrs clinging to his clothing—and his dog! When trying to remove them, he was impressed (and probably a bit frustrated!) at how strongly the burrs hung on. He became curious about how burrs worked and he wondered if he could mimic nature's very effective attachment system in a way that humans could use.

It took eight years of trying, but de Mestral finally succeeded. His invention involved using two strips of fabric. One strip had thousands of tiny hooks. The other strip had thousands of tiny loops. Press them together and…presto! Millions of kids could fasten their own shoes! Plus, an international corporation with all kinds of useful products was born.

Success stories like Velcro™ motivate **biotechnology engineers** to invent new products. They look to nature for ideas about how to keep people and the planet healthy. Jellyfish, geckos, bees, butterflies, and fireflies are just a few of nature's creatures inspiring big new ideas.

Biotech has already introduced many wow-worthy products. Plastic bottles made

Ask Big Questions!

Go outside to look for biotech inspiration. **What do you see in nature that could be used to make or inspire a new product?** Sketch out your idea and give it a name.

from wheat, corn, or potatoes are one cool biotech innovation. Other awesome products with amazing potential are lifesaving medicines for certain types of cancer. Engineers are also using natural substances, like algae or sugarcane, to make alternative fuels.

Some engineers are even looking at ways for humans to ingest information through the bloodstream. If that happens, you could swallow a pill to study for a test. "Bring it on," say students everywhere!

Creative biotech engineers will continue to find wonderful ways to put science to work with life-changing ideas and products.

Explore Some More!

Cells? Microbes? Plants? Animals? It's all there at **www.biology4kids.com**.

Did you know that nearly half of the prescribed drugs used in the United States come from rainforest plants?

Cyber Security Agent

ection

Cyber security

Surf the 'Net!

Bullies aren't just on playgrounds anymore. You can find them online too. Learn how to spot and stop online bullying by searching for information about **cyberbullies for kids**.

Pretend you have a crush on a classmate. You really like him or her. You are pretty sure he or she likes you back. How can you find out for sure? You could just ask in person, but someone could hear you and blab the news all over the school. This is top-secret stuff! Sending an e-mail is the only way to keep it private. Or is it?

Businesses and governments also need to keep their secrets safe. Stopping bad people from misusing technology prevents lots of bad things. Spies cannot steal product ideas from other companies. Criminals cannot break into power grids and cause dangerous black-outs. Terrorists can't use cyberspace to plot attacks. People's banking and credit card information is kept safe from identity theft.

Cyber security agents stop or solve **cybercrimes**. Since almost every business, government, and individual uses technology these days, demand is high for cyber security experts of all kinds. The Federal Bureau of Investigation (FBI) says that cybercrime is one of its top law enforcement challenges. The U.S. government spends billions of dollars trying to prevent cybercrime.

It can be bad news when **hackers** break into corporate computer systems. In 2013, hackers broke into the computer systems of a big department store chain called Target, and stole credit and debit card information on 40 million customers. It was big news and a big problem for the customers and Target stores everywhere.

Ask Big Questions!

What are some ways you can keep yourself and your friends safe online? Make up a personal, online safety checklist to share with your classmates.

Explore Some More!

Visit the **FBI Cyber Surf Island** online at **sos.fbi. gov/new-main-page** for some adventures in cyber security.

It cost the retailer over $162 million to fix the problem. They are still working hard to rebuild their reputation as a safe place to shop.

Cyber warfare has become so common that the U.S. military established a cyber command to combat it. An entire division of cyber experts work night and day to keep the nation safe from cyber attacks.

Even schools and families like yours find it necessary to take precautions against hackers, **malware**, and other threats to online privacy. When it's done correctly the message is clear:

Hackers beware!

Most credit cards are now fitted with a small, metallic, high-tech chip to prevent thieves from stealing consumers' personal information.

Data Scientist

Big data is like the modern version of the nineteenth-century California Gold Rush. Forget panning for gold in the Wild West. **Data scientists** dig for golden opportunities hiding in information from a variety of sources.

Data scientists use a mix of computer programming and math skills. They start by gathering, organizing, and analyzing different kinds of information. Then they look for ways to mix the data

Surf the 'Net!

Have fun playing around with math by searching for online math games for kids.

to help businesses solve problems and create opportunities. Creativity counts when it comes to big data. Finding interesting connections is where data scientists hit pay dirt!

For instance, hotels want to fill their vacant rooms. That's how they earn money and stay in business. Let's say you own a hotel near a big airport. There are bound to be days when people get stranded there due to bad weather. So you link data about bad weather with data about flight cancellations and weary travelers. Then when weather hits, you send out social media alerts offering a special discount for stranded passengers. The problem is solved for the travelers—plus, there's new business for your hotel. Sweet dreams!

Retail stores, like Macy's, use big data to keep track of prices and sales on the millions of products they carry. When data shows a certain product is selling like hotcakes, store executives know to order more. When a product isn't selling so well, it's time to discount

Ask Big Questions!

Learn about your eating habits by keeping track of what you eat for a week. **What does the data tell you about making healthy choices?** Make a chart that compares your good and, um, not so good choices.

the price! Big data helps executives keep track of supply and demand.

Big data is everywhere! Police departments use it to predict where crimes are most likely to occur. Schools use it to help teachers individualize instruction. Professional sports teams are in on the big data game too. They use it to make decisions about game strategy.

It might be true that you, like most kids, don't exactly dream of growing up to be data scientists. But it is worth thinking about. The field is growing like crazy, and data scientists can earn as much as doctors or lawyers earn. Who knows? You might strike gold as a future data scientist!

Explore Some More!

Probability is probably more interesting than you think! See for yourself at **www.studyjams. scholastic.com**.

Data scientists collect data from many different sources and use charts to share their findings.

E-commerce Manager

Cha-Ching! That's the sound of billions of dollars rolling in for online retailers. For more and more Americans, the Internet is becoming the place to shop 'til you drop. With a click of a mouse—and credit card info—you can buy anything from airline tickets and automobiles to designer fashion, and even, um, toilet paper.

No worries though! Brick-and-mortar stores (that's what they call the retailers you visit in person) are here to stay too.

Surf the 'Net!

Look up the **name of your favorite store**, and visit its online website. For instance, search for **Apple** to see the latest in cell phones and tablets. Or check out trendy new sneakers at **Nike**.

Hanging out at the local mall is just way too much fun. Besides, there are times when you don't know you want a product until you see it on the shelf. But there are times when the convenience of shopping from your home computer just can't be beat.

That's why most retail brands have stores you can visit in person and online. Amazon, the biggest online retailer of them all, does business only online. (At least for now.) Thousands of small retailers also find online success by offering unique, hard-to-find products to national and international audiences. There are even online stores, like eBay, where millions of people sell all kinds of stuff—old and new.

All this online retail keeps **e-commerce managers** busy. They set up online storefronts, market websites, and use social media to keep in touch with customers. Setting up safe and efficient payment systems is one of their most important jobs. Then there's the matter of processing orders and managing inventory.

E-commerce is big, big business!

Ask Big Questions!

What kinds of online stores appeal to kids your age? Answer this question in pictures by making a collage of images from kid-friendly websites.

Explore Some More!

Find out how much Americans are spending on their favorite products online every second at **www.retale.com/info/retail-in-real-time**. Hint: It's a lot!

Online shopping lets customers shop to their heart's content from the comfort of their own homes.

Companies with a big online presence have entire staffs of people who specialize in various types of e-commerce skills. Big or small, it's all about getting customers to the site, treating them well, and getting them coming back for more.

It will be interesting to see how e-commerce continues to evolve. One big challenge is getting products to customers more quickly. Some think that drones may one day be used to deliver orders to customers.

It's a bird! It's a plane! No, it's not Superman. It's high-tech special delivery!

Mobile App Designer

Surf the 'Net!

Try out some fun, **free online games** offered by kid-friendly websites like **PBS Kids**, **Disney**, and **Nickelodeon**.

So you want to keep track of your fitness activities? There's an **app** for that. You want to learn to speak a foreign language? There are apps for that! Or do you need to find out more about your favorite sport? There are plenty of terrific apps for that too!

As a matter of fact, there are apps for just about anything you imagine. At last count, both the Google Play Store and the Apple App Store offered more than 1.5 million apps. Behind every one of those apps are **mobile app designers** who came up with the ideas and program the computer code that makes the apps work.

Of course, there are so many apps that you might wonder why anyone needs to design another one. Don't worry. By the time you get old enough to work as a mobile app designer, many current apps will be obsolete. There will be newer, faster, better technologies to make apps more useful and more fun.

Plus, there will be even more opportunities to make life better for people around the world. Some mobile app designers are busy creating apps that change, or even save, lives.

Some apps bring learning and education to places where schools aren't available. These apps help teach children and adults to read and write. Or they educate people about health care and nutrition. In these cases, technology truly saves the day by providing information and skills people need to lead better lives.

Ask Big Questions!

Can you think of an idea for an app that would make learning fun for people your age? Sketch out your ideas and list all of the things kids could do with the app.

Other apps create ways for people to run businesses and earn a living for their families. For instance, in Africa, M-Pesa (which means "mobile money" in Swahili) has made day-to-day banking possible for millions of people in rural areas who don't have access to traditional banks. iCow is a popular mobile app that helps dairy farmers manage their cows more sustainably.

Mobile apps aren't just for goofing off—although there is plenty of room for fun. Mobile technologies have the potential to solve real problems too. Make the world a better place? There's an app for that!

Explore Some More!

Create your own stories, games, and animations online at **scratch.mit. edu**.

Computer apps are changing the way children learn all over the world.

Nanotechnologist

Surf the 'Net!

Find **videos** about **how nanotechnology works**. Be prepared to be amazed!

They say good things come in small packages. **Nanotechnologists** are sure to agree. These specialists are scientists and engineers who work with some of the world's smallest particles, called "**nanometers**," to create incredible new products.

How small is a nanometer? It's so small you can't see it with your eyes or touch it with your hands. You can't even see it with a regular microscope. A nanometer measures about one-billionth of a meter. To compare, one sheet of paper is about one hundred thousand nanometers thick. Nanometers take small to a whole new level!

Why is smallness such a big deal? Nanotechnology scientists and engineers are discovering that "small" can do things "big" cannot. Working on a small scale helps them create new materials, molecule-by-molecule. This ultra-precise process unlocks properties and powers that aren't available through traditional means.

If this sounds complicated, it is because it is very complicated. Yet nanotechnology is already used to solve some rather simple problems. Take sunscreen, for instance. Two ingredients—zinc oxide and titanium dioxide—help reflect or absorb cancer-causing ultraviolet light.

Some sunscreens are made with ingredients larger than nanometers, but sunscreens made with nano-sized

Ask Big Questions!

Let's say you were to wake up one morning to discover you are 100,000 times smaller than you were the night before. **What kinds of things could you do in this teeny-tiny size that you couldn't as a regular-size kid?** Write a story about your adventures!

Explore Some More!

Enter the Nanozone at **www.nanozone.org**.

particles of the same ingredients work better. For one thing, smaller particles absorb not only ultraviolet light, but they absorb and scatter visible light too. A big bonus is that this sunscreen rubs into your skin more easily and doesn't leave you looking like a ghost. Nanotechnology took a good product and made it even better.

The potential of nanotechnology is getting bigger all the time. Medicine, agriculture, and industry are big areas of nanotechnology activity. Imagine a day when medicine contains tiny nanorobots programmed to attack cancer cells. That's just one of the big ideas waiting to be tackled by future nanotechnologists.

Nanotechnologists are exploring amazing new ways to deliver medicines to patients with life-threatening diseases like cancer.

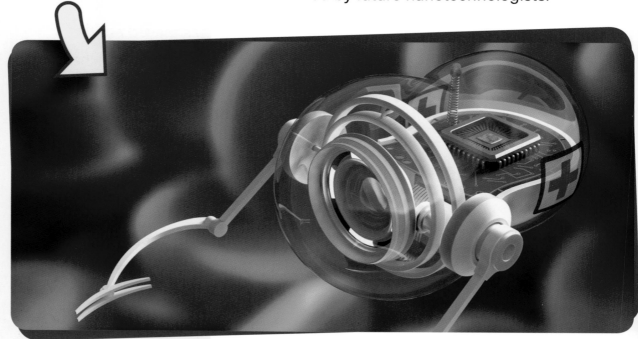

Video Game Designer

Surf the 'Net!

Search the name of your favorite video game. Look at the company's website to find out all you can about how the game was made.

Xbox, Nintendo, Disney Infinity, free online video games, and games played on kids' television websites—all these games have at least one thing in common. What is it? Lots and lots of people spend lots and lots of time playing them!

In fact, there are about 155 million **gamers** in the United States alone. They spend an average of six and a half hours a week playing video games. Guess what? The average age of gamers is thirty-five! It's not just kids who are playing games. Adults like to have fun too!

Video game designers get paid to keep all these gamers happy. They create games that involve strategy, sports, adventure, role-playing, and lots and lots of action.

Think about your favorite game. What makes it so much fun? Is it the characters? The story? The challenge to move up to higher levels? Chances are your answers to these questions are yes, yes, and yes.

Can you imagine how much work it takes to create a blockbuster game? Top-selling video games can cost over $20 million to create. Some cost upwards of $100 million to develop. That's how much it takes to pay all the designers, programmers, writers, artists, and testers who create layer upon layer of action. It takes a lot of time and money to create a game that provides for hour upon hour of enjoyment.

Of course, games that get it right make the investment well worth the time and effort. Minecraft is one of the best-selling

Ask Big Questions!

What does it take to make a video game that kids like you will want to play again and again? Play one of your favorite classic board games with a friend and figure out how you could punch up the strategy and rules to make it into a video game. Make an advertisement touting your ideas to entice gamers to play.

games of all time, earning over $700 million. The game has been downloaded one hundred million times...and counting! In fact, the word "Minecraft" is Googled more often than the Bible, Harry Potter, and famous pop stars!

Things like virtual reality and artificial intelligence are sure to make video games of the future even more exciting. Games will keep getting more immersive and realistic than ever.

One of the best ways to prepare to become a video game designers is to spend time playing video games. If only your parents would agree!

Explore Some More!

Go behind the scenes to find out how video games are made at **electronics. howstuffworks.com/ making-a-video-game. htm**.

Some video games let gamers create new worlds to play in.

Find *Your* Future in Technology

Let's review the amazing career ideas you've just discovered. Below are descriptions of some of the opportunities waiting for people who like technology. Read the sentences below and match the description with the career it describes.

Instead of writing in this book, use a separate sheet of paper to write your answers. Even better, download a free activity sheet at www.cherrylakepublishing.com/activities.

A Artificial intelligence scientist

B Biotechnology engineer

C Cyber security agent

D Data scientist

E E-commerce manager

F Mobile app designer

G Nanotechnologist

H Video game designer

1 Figuring out a system to schedule drone deliveries of your online store's products

2 Unraveling the secrets of how worms regrow after amputation in order to develop human organs that can heal themselves

3 Using nanoparticles to create a test that can detect cancer cells before tumors can be seen in X-rays

4 Using big data to pick the winning lineup for the champion Super Bowl football team

5 Using virtual reality to create a game that lets gamers travel back in time

6 Creating an app that warns people of earthquakes and other natural disasters before they happen

7 Stopping a ring of cybercriminals who plan to disrupt the subway transportation system in a major U.S. city

8 Inventing a robot that can help kids with their homework and household chores

(Answer Key: 1-E; 2-B; 3-G; 4-D; 5-H; 6-F; 7-C; 8-A)

Glossary

algorithm procedure or formula used in mathematics and computer science to solve problems

app specialized program, or application, people download onto mobile devices

artificial intelligence scientist person who uses science and engineering to make intelligent machines

biotechnology engineer person who uses biological processes to make new products

Cortana a digital assistant found on Microsoft products

cybercrime crime committed by way of the Internet or other computer network

cybersecurity agent expert who uses technology to fight cyber crime and protect cyberspace

data scientist person who works with large amounts of data, to help a business gain a competitive edge

digital native person born after the use of computers, the Internet, and other digital technologies became widespread

e-commerce manager person who runs or manages various aspects of an online business

gamer person who plays computer games

global positioning system (GPS) a satellite-powered navigation system that allows people to determine their exact location at any given time and in all weather conditions

hacker person who uses computers to gain unauthorized access to data and computer systems

malware software intended to damage or disable computers and computer systems

mobile app designer person who designs and develops software applications for digital devices such as cell phones and tablets

nanometer a unit of measurement that is one-billionth of a meter

nanotechnologist scientist or engineer who work with materials on an atomic or molecular scale, especially to build microscopic devices and other products

robotics the branch of engineering and computer science that deals with robots

Siri a digital assistant found on Apple technology products

video game designer person who designs and develops digital games for entertainment and educational purposes

Index

About the Author

Diane Lindsey Reeves is the author of lots of children's books. She has written several original PEANUTS stories (published by Regnery Kids and Sourcebooks). She is especially curious about what people do, and she likes to write books that get kids thinking about all the cool things they can be when they grow up. She lives in Cary, North Carolina, and her favorite thing to do is play with her grandkids — Conrad, Evan, Reid, and Hollis Grace.